The
Fireside
Book
2023

"In prosperity our friends know us; in adversity we know our friends."
– *John Churton Collins*

Contents

Poetry

From The Manse Window

Nature's Calendar

Illustrations by Manon Gandiolle and Mandy Dixon.

The Merry Months Of Spring

The months of spring are here at last,
Winter days are fading fast,
Nature's joy pervades the air,
Sweet life renewing everywhere!

Mad March hares box and tease
And lambs are leaping in the leas,
Flowers are bursting forth divine:
Primrose, crocus, celandine.

In April, Easter bonnets grace
Ladies wearing bright new lace,
Bluebells carpet woodland floors;
What a joy to be outdoors!

In the very merry month of May
Around the maypole dance all day,
Whilst the cuckoo sings his song
On warmer breezes all day long.

George Hughes

Bulb Planting

Bulbs and compost, trowels and gloves,
That's everything we need.
"Can we start now, Grandma?"
Excited voices plead.

We plant them deep inside the pots,
Just five in every one.
The children work with eager hands
And soon our task is done.

In January's chilly days,
The tiny shoots we see.
Then as the sun gets stronger
The yellow buds break free.

Though I've seen before those tiny bulbs
Transformed to trumpets tall,
Still I join the children's wonder
At the magic of it all.

Kate Bradbury

The Weather House

There's a wooden alpine chalet fixed to my granny's wall.
I can't quite reach to touch it because I'm only small.
The little wooden house has a secret, I can tell,
For when the weather changes, the chalet does as well.
Two tiny people live inside it – a woman and a man.
The man holds an umbrella, the woman holds a fan.
They have a special job to do, which means they never meet,
For when it rains the man pops out, but the woman must retreat.
She just comes out to see the sun
But then the man must turn and run,
How sad it always is to see,
Never face to face to be.
Perhaps one day, if the fates decide,
They will be happy, side by side.

Frances Pankiewicz

Motherhood

I checked the morning you were born
Each finger, nail and thumb,
Amazed that after all the pain
I'd finally become "Mum".

As time went on you used those hands
To grasp at many things,
From knives and forks and writing pens
To handlebars and swings.

You held my hand to cross the road,
A tight but welcome grip,
And waved away the nerves to bravely
Go on your school trip.

Dad later walked you down the aisle
To give your hand away.
Although I shed a tear or two
I smiled so much that day.

And now we're kissing your own baby's
Precious hands and feet,
The circle of my motherhood
Is beautifully complete.

Laura Tapper

The Rainy Wood

There's something rather wonderful
About a rainy wood –
That fresh green smell just fills the lungs
And turns bad moods to good!
The drip, drip, drip of leaves and shrubs,
The soft wind's gentle sigh,
That strange grey light confuses time
Beneath the heavy sky.
And cobwebs, normally unseen,
Are lit with neon light
As drops bejewel every strand
To make them shine so bright.
So if the world feels all too much
And efforts seem in vain,
Just don your wellies, find some trees
And walk there in the rain!

Eileen Hay

iStock.

The Right Time

MY favourite time to travel is in the spring, but in this country only, not abroad. I would never go abroad in April or May. There is no more beautiful place on earth than the UK in springtime.

The opening line of Robert Browning's poem, "Oh, to be in England now that April's there", resonates deep within my soul.

My heart sings for joy when I see the tracery of lime and apple-green new leaves on trees, the wash of cream hawthorn blossom and magnolia, pink cherry blossom and swathes of bluebells in hedgerows and hidden fields.

And there is very little that compares with the dawn chorus. The world is new and the whole of summer lies ahead.

Yet these very things cause me to stress out, too. When exactly is the best time to book that trip?

If I go too early, then I might miss the bluebells and the blossom; too late and everything will have gone over.

I once drove to the Forest of Dean for the day because I'd heard there were carpets of bluebells, only to find when I arrived that there was barely a flower to be seen because it had been a cold start to the season and they hadn't put in an appearance yet.

Because spring only comes once a year, and we wait so long for it, I want to squeeze every last bit out of it and everything has to fall into place.

Sometimes timing is everything, and trying to get it perfect can cause a measure of anxiety.

When it comes to the bigger things in life, things more important than whether I get to see the bluebells or not, it's good to know that God is sovereign and that his timing is always right, even when we don't necessarily see it.

The Apostle Paul writes to the church in Rome:

"You see, at just the right time, when we were still powerless, Christ died for the ungodly." (Romans 5:6 NIV)

And to the churches in

By Rev. Susan Sarapuk

Galatia he wrote:

"When the time had fully come, God sent his son, born of a woman, born under law, to redeem those under law, that we might receive the full rights of sons." (Galatians 4:4-5 NIV)

We had no say or control over these things happening – how could we, when it was over 2,000 years ago?

Yet God was perfectly in control and had a plan that would affect us today.

He still knows what's right for us.

I left full-time ministry over 10 years ago and settled back into my home parish, where I helped to take services, lead worship and assist with bible study.

On a couple of occasions there could have been an opportunity to become vicar, and I really felt I would like to take it on.

I prayed about it, waited for God, but on neither of those occasions did the door open.

With hindsight I can understand why: how would I have coped with having to do online ministry?

Unforeseen circumstances have led to the closure of the parish church until funds can be raised for essential maintenance, and I would have really struggled with leadership in that situation.

God knows what we are capable of. He saw what I couldn't see.

We like to be in charge and make our own decisions. James writes about this in his letter:

"Now listen you who say, 'today or tomorrow we will go to this or that city, spend a year there, carry on business, make money'.

"Why, you do not even know what will happen tomorrow. What is your life? You are a mist that appears for a little while and then vanishes." (James 4: 13-14. NIV)

In the Old Testament, God promised David that the kingdom would be his one day. A couple of times David had Saul at his mercy, yet chose not to take advantage of that.

He refused to soil his hands and his conscience as a murderer of the lord's anointed, and waited for God's timing, when God delivered the kingdom to him.

In contrast, when Saul was a newly anointed King, he was told to wait for the prophet Samuel to turn up to offer sacrifice before the army went out to battle the Philistines.

When Samuel did not arrive at the appointed time, Saul decided to go ahead and offer the sacrifice himself. Samuel turned up at the end and rebuked him.

The foundation of Saul's reign was impatience and a lack of trust, whereas David, for all his faults, was a man after God's own heart.

We live in a society where personal choice and self-gratification are highly prized. Why wait for something if it's there and you have the chance to grab it?

We've all made rash decisions that we've come to regret. Often they were driven by an overwhelming desire, and nothing was going to stop us, not even God.

I expect, like me, that you've shut him off because you don't want to hear.

By his grace and mercy, even our wilful mistakes can be rectified and turned to good if we allow him to work. Things always work out best in his timing.

These days, when I look around at a society and church I often no longer recognise, I'm tempted to despair.

I remember then what a wise Christian friend often says: "God is in control; he'll sort it out."

That doesn't mean we should sit back and do nothing. What it does mean, in the words of one of my favourite hymns is: "God is working his purpose out as year succeeds to year", and his timing is perfect.

I'm not in charge of the church or the state.

Catching the bluebells at the right time will always be hit or miss – we can never tell from one year to the next if spring is going to be early or late.

One thing is certain – God is always on time. His time. ■

Nature's Calendar For Spring

In Season: Sorrel

Sorrel grows in the UK all year. Full of vitamin C and fibre, it can be used for salads in summer and made into a soup for cold weather. It has a fruity flavour that can bring soups and stews to life as a garnish or extra addition.

On The Farm: Lambing Time

Farmers will be on hand around the clock for signs of any trouble. First-time mums are normally kept close by and inside for safe-keeping. It's important that lambs are up quickly and feeding from their mums as soon as possible.

World Forestry Day

March 21 has been declared a day to celebrate woodlands by the UN. Forests are the lungs of the world, yet we lose an area the size of Iceland to deforestation each year. Forests are vital for the health of the planet, and are important for mental health, too, as we're finding out.

Shutterstock.

Tree Life: Budburst

Buds on trees indicate the imminent arrival of leaves or blossom. The tree has detected the oncoming of warmer weather, though scientists have discovered that light pollution in cities causes trees to bud earlier. This effect is compounded by the fact that urban areas are usually warmer than rural locations.

Brown Hare Boxing

If you're lucky, you might spot brown hares boxing in the bare fields of early spring. Unusually, it's unlikely to be two males fighting, but a female trying to ward off unwelcome advances from a male. Brown hares are Britain's fastest land mammals.

In Season: Artichoke

Packed with thiamin, niacin and iron, artichokes are a winter veg that are still in season as spring rolls around. Depending on the kind of weather March brings, they can be cut into chunks and roasted like potatoes, puréed and added to hearty soups and warming risottos, or braised and added to a salad.

The Driving Instructor

It's a funny old job, teaching people to drive,
Hoping today I'll get home alive!
Bunny hops, wrong turns, not turning the key,
And that's not my students – that's just me!

From the very start it can be quite tough;
Some students find first gear enough
To make them panic and get in a tizz –
"I'm going too fast!" screams my student Liz.

With gentle advice she steers round the bend,
But forgets to straighten when she comes to the end.
My hand on the wheel, heart in my mouth,
I manage to stop it from all going south.

"Yippee! I'm a driver," Liz says with a smile,
Although we're yet to complete a mile.
"You're doing so well." (There's sweat on my palm!)
"Now let's try second." (I will remain calm!)

And so we progress, honing her skill;
She can now get going while on a hill.
Liz learns to reverse and park the car –
A few weeks later we're going quite far.

Before we know it, it's time for the test,
And all I can do is wish her the best.
It's all in her hands, no more can I do,
On to my next student – I bid her adieu.

She did it – she passed! She's very pleased, too.
"Thank you!" she says. "It's all down to you."
My job here is done and I'm still alive!
It's a funny old job, teaching people to drive.

Hester Jimpson

The Pigeon

In my garden, in a tree,
A pigeon built a nest;
The way she sits there, day by day,
Has left me most impressed.
Her nest is not far from the ground,
A place I daily tread,
Beneath a birch's silvery branch,
And just above my head.
I watch her from my window
When having friends to tea;
That's why I let my trees grow wild,
For the joy they give to me.

Lots of trees mean lots of birds,
And mine grow close together;
They lift the heart on summer days,
The same in wintry weather.
And so the cycle works around,
The pleasure never ends;
And soon – when these new eggs have hatched –
I'll be having more new friends.

Dawn Lawrence

You're Welcome

We're on our Easter outing
With picnic lunch in tow.
It isn't raining, isn't blowing,
Just a lovely springtime show.
We're settled on the riverbank,
The bees are buzzing by,
While in the bluest blue
A blackbird beats the sky.
There are vistas of velvet green,
Of glade and lime and mint,
Sweet fresh earth, that herbal scent,
Such charms on Easter's brink.
Now reverence is taken up
With the birds in hallowed song,
And the horses, cows and sheep
Happy, where they belong.
The search is on for hidden eggs,
Chocolate rabbits are on the shelf,
Easter's cards sent with best wishes,
Proclaiming all her wealth.

Dorothy McGregor

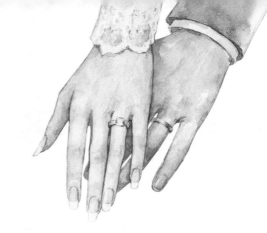

Wedding Registrar

What could be nicer than being in love
And wanting to make that love true
By joining together in matrimony
And placing your trust in "I do"?
And I am the person who's privileged enough
To guide them through pledging their vows.
I see the pure joy that a wedding can give,
The happiest of days it allows.
Families' faces are flushed and excited,
The bride and the groom are aglow,
Bridesmaids are flustered and Grandma is crying
(But trying hard to not let it show).
The bride is so lovely, the groom is so proud,
As the bouquet is tossed in the air . . .
Now my part is done, I'm off to the next one,
There's no better job anywhere!

Linda Brown

East Coast Wanderings

There may not be big mountains, nor rugged hills to climb,
Yet there is indeed a beauty which people think sublime.
Meander through small woodlands, where bird song will enchant,
And search along the seashore for dune-grown spiky plants.

Small round holes riddle the cliffs, sand pipers come to nest;
Darting back and forwards, they barely seem to rest.
Slatted wooden bridges straddle a trickling stream –
Stop awhile, inhale the peace, enjoy this pleasant scene.

The broads are full of wildlife, from reedbeds to hedgerow,
Marsh harriers soar regally, while shy deer graze below.
Step lightly where small lizards seek the morning sun.
Leave nothing but odd footprints and remember to have fun.

Angie Keeler

With Good Intentions

A border collie, Brynley was,
But a puppy all the same –
So he was only learning
This so called "herding" game.

Bryn was making progress,
And all went on quite well
Until the day when – oh, dear me! –
I hardly dare to tell.

The farmer, as his master,
Should hang his head in shame;
It was due to his forgetfulness,
So he should take the blame.

The field gate left wide open
Left Bryn with several choices;
No doubt within his doggy mind
He heard conflicting voices.

But having once decided,
He set to work with zest,
So glad he'd solved the problem
And convinced he'd passed the test.

The farmhouse, close and handy,
Was the best place he could find,
And with the front door open
The lounge soon came to mind.

Imagine, then, the farmer's plight,
His shocked, confounded stare,
To find about a hundred sheep
All huddled, bleating there!

And Bryn, with good intentions,
Sat there with obvious pride,
As if to say, "Look what I've done –
I've penned them all inside!"

Dawn Lawrence

Little Pink Cottage

Little pink cottage –
It's where I call home,
So dear to my heart,
Where I'm happy alone.

Little pink cottage,
Your walls hold my fears.
You know all my worries,
I trust your kind ears.

I'm warmed by your fire,
I've cried at your hearth,
Pondered life's mysteries –
Love, life, death and birth.

You've shared in my secrets,
Had wind of my dreams,
Heard my quiet whispers;
My guardian, it seems.

More than bricks and mortar,
Seen me laugh, made me smile.
You're encased in my heart
So I'm staying a while.

Tina MacNaughton

iStock.

from the Manse Window

Colour Me Spring

O N my fortieth birthday, many moons ago now, I was given an unusual gift. It was a voucher for Colour Me Beautiful, of which I had never heard.

This treat involved a trip to a pretty farmhouse in the middle of the Dumfriesshire countryside and a session with a lovely lady who gave me coffee and scones.

A good start!

My analyst explained to me that many women not only wear the wrong shape of clothing but, more importantly, the wrong colour.

She looked at my skin and eye colour, taking into account my rosy cheeks, then proceeded to swathe me in large pieces of fabric.

This was intriguing as I began to see that my usual fawns, light browns and creams were actually very draining. It did take a while to convince me that I would look good in purple.

Jenny Joseph, in her poem "Warning", did indeed recommend the wearing of purple in old age.

However, I surmised that this advice was more to shock and to show defiance than to look

particularly good!

Originally, Colour Me Beautiful analysts would categorise their clients as being spring, summer, autumn or winter.

I had been dressing for years as an autumn and on this day discovered that I was, in fact, a spring!

My new friend gave me a little wallet to carry around when I went shopping, showing the spring shades which suited me best.

She also told me that I should wear gold and not silver.

I did mention this to my husband, but I am still waiting to prove if this is the case!

After my session I went to spend my birthday money and some savings I had gathered.

I could hardly believe it when I saw a beautiful purple skirt, a similarly striped top and an anorak in my favourite store.

I decided to go the whole hog, and also purchased a soft jade skirt, another of my new colours.

Wow, what a transformation!

My family were all very impressed with the new look. ▶

By Janice Ross

But what was interesting was the response of my class of eight-year-olds.

"Mrs Ross, you look beautiful today!"

I would like to say that I changed that day from being an autumn person to a spring person.

Sadly, character and temperament are not so easy to transform as outward appearances.

What, I wonder, might a spring person be like?

For many, spring is the favourite season of the year.

The dark, dreich days of wind and rain, often from November through to February (at least in Scotland), give way to a little more daylight and the promise of new life in the garden.

The light greens of new leaves, the purples of crocus, hyacinths and primula denticulata, the creams and purple pink of fritillaria are all so welcome, lifting our spirits.

There is hope in the coming of spring, hope of new beginnings, hope of breakthrough.

In the natural realm, all through the darkness of winter, life has been stirring.

Deep in the earth, fallen acorns sprout first roots and shoots, which then slowly weave and thread their way to the surface, to stretch out to the brightness of daylight.

Have you ever marvelled at a little shoot forcing its way through a crack in concrete and cement?

These tiny dormant seeds can't help themselves. They were made to live.

So a spring person might be a person of hope.

For a Christian, the Bible gives us many things of which we are assured: God's unfailing love for us, his children; his forgiveness through the cross of Easter; his presence when we are going through the hard times of life.

Having hope in God means grasping these truths with both hands and proving them in our lives.

It also means blessing others with our positive attitudes.

Spring also speaks to me of faithfulness. God is the one who changes times and the seasons.

His word says that spring is coming and that winter will pass. Dark days, harsh weather and gloomy spirits can be lifted.

Bulbs will again push through the earth, daffodils will again raise their golden heads, once again garden birds will waken us with joyful song and geese will herald the coming of the season.

Spring reminds us of God's faithfulness in bringing us through darkness and into light.

Sometimes we have to tell our weary souls to embrace light and life, to breathe in the freshness of new life and by doing so prove to be a blessing to others.

In "Fisherman's Luck" by Henry Van Dyke, the poet observed that "the first day of spring is one thing, and the first spring day is another."

Spring can indeed be a time of many showers.

The wise king Solomon in the book of Proverbs likened God's favour "to a raincloud in spring."

New flowers appearing need the showers of early spring – and children appear to enjoy them, too!

Isn't it strange that we don't object so much to the rain of April as we do to the rain of November or February?

I think a spring person might be one who, if her life feels like a dried-up desert, knows how to reach up in faith to the Lord in prayer for his springtime showers of blessing.

I'd like to think that she would be one to bring lightness, laughter and joy to others.

My colouring has definitely changed with age. My hair is now quite grey. I have given up wearing purples and jades, and my shape has certainly changed for the worse!

I am not sure what a colour analyst's recommendations would be today. As I am now retired, I wouldn't be able to go out and buy a new wardrobe, either.

And I am still waiting for some gold accessories.

Perhaps it would be silver that would suit me better nowadays? Now that would be a pity! ■

Nature's Calendar For Spring

International Dawn Chorus Day

May 1 celebrates the birdsong that greets us in the early morning, and at his time of year it's pretty early in the morning. In late spring, the birds are giving it their all because they're either defending their territory or seeking a new mate!

In Season: Watercress

One of Britain's native superfoods, watercress is packed with vitamins, has more calcium than milk and more potassium than a banana! It's relatively low on food miles as well, as buying this in season will likely mean it's come from the sunny south of the UK.

The Basking Shark Is Back!

The basking shark returns to UK waters in May. It's not a threat to humans as it feeds only on small fish and plankton! It spends winter near the Caribbean and Florida. This was a mystery until recently, when they were found overwintering in the warmer seas.

In Season: Elderflowers

The last days of spring see elderflowers reach their finest and freshest. Picked on a warm, dry day, they can be added to a few simple ingredients (and some sugar) to create cordial. If you're foraging for your own, it's best — as with any hedgerow pickings — to avoid those beside busy roads, as the fumes and dirt will affect their quality.

On The Farm: Cleaning Out

As the animals return to the fields, it's a great time to clean out the sheds they've spent the winter in. Pressure washing the dirt and grime that accumulates after a winter indoors is a vital job to prevent any nasties growing indoors. Plus it's a chance to check for any winter damage. Not a fun job, but it needs doing!

Tree Life: First Leaf

Leaves feed trees by photosynthesis. The chlorophyll that gives them their green colour converts sunlight (along with water and carbon dioxide) into sugars that the tree uses to sustain itself and grow. At this time of year, the first leaves will be appearing on some trees, while others may take longer to arrive.

A Refreshing Walk

The lichen on the branches of contorted apple trees,
Like gold and khaki daubs of paint, stay static in the breeze,
While ballerina blossoms, with their raspberry sorbet hems,
Pirouette and arabesque above the hawthorn stems.
The dappled shade, along the path that myriad feet have known,
Veils cowslip crouching in the verge where grass is overgrown.
The bluebells dress the woodland trail with beads of azure hue,
But violets can scarce be seen as I weave on and through
The five-bar gate which draws me down to pause beside the stream,
Where sun-kissed boulders beckon me to rest, reflect and dream.

Carol Brindley

Racing Fun

Can we have a race," my toddler son asks.
I take tiny, slow steps so he thinks that he's fast.

"Can we have a race?" my eight-year-old begs.
I must take my time as he still has small legs.

"Can we have a race?" my twelve-year- old pleads.
Although it's a struggle, I'm still in the lead.

"Can we have a race?" My teenage son laughs.
With new lanky legs, he runs like a giraffe.

"Can we have a race?" my grown son I ask.
Note his small steps to let me think I'm fast!

Lily Christie

Green With Envy

A garden, I've discovered,
Reveals the simple truth
Of how it's found the secret of
Eternal, blooming youth.
No matter if it's stood for years,
Overgrown, neglected,
Through skilful horticultural hands
It's quickly resurrected.

Some annuals or herbaceous plants
Can soon the weeds replace,
Their colours very similar to
Make-up on a face.
If only it could be the same
For people as for flowers;
A rich, top soil transfusion
Restoring all our powers.

Though years may leave their mark on us
As we slip past our prime,
A garden in its glory is like
Stepping back in time.

John Darley

Scents Of Summer

Ripe strawberries and new-mown grass,
And perfume in the air
Of roses, sweetpeas, lavender,
That make the senses flare.
Each season has its own sweet scents –
In spring, fresh daffodils,
And autumn's wood smoke makes us think
Of coming winter chills.
But summer scents bring happy thoughts
Of picnics by the sea,
Or city parks with summer blooms
And children running free.
When air is warm it smells so sweet
And lifts our spirits high –
The song of birds, the fresh green grass,
Above, a clear blue sky.

Eileen Hay

Caterpillar Crisis

Caterpillar, caterpillar, munching on that leaf –
Now, should I let you linger there, or will you cause me grief?
I fear, if I should let you stay, my cabbages you'll eat,
And yet, although it's strange to say, I find you rather sweet.
You wriggle with such purpose that I'm sure you have a plot,
Perhaps to find my veggie beds, and scoff the whole darn lot!
So caterpillar, listen, if I choose to let you stay,
Please promise you'll eat just one leaf, and then you'll go away!

Maggie Ingall

The Language Of Trees

Trees live their lives in the slow lane,
Even when danger is near,
But deep down when roots are in trouble
The messages soon become clear.
All different parts are alerted
To trigger the leaves to respond,
And their special scent is the language
That they use to converse, and to bond.

Their scent is distributed widely,
Though quickly dispersed in the air,
But creatures detect the alarm calls
And know when to take extra care.
Old mother trees are the leaders,
Their trunks stretching out to the sky
Like columns in a cathedral,
Standing guard as the years roll by.

Tree parents live close together,
Supporting their young as they grow,
Sharing nutrients with all those who struggle,
A fact which most people don't know.
So when walking out in the woodland,
Think well on the nature of trees –
You might find the signs and signals received
Are not always due to the breeze.

Dawn Lawrence

The High Farm

After winding the hill one stands back,
Blown out. A buzzard prowls, a skate of air,
Bending over the rush of trees. Summer.
And the river browses fallow through restless fields.

At the high farm, a dog flames out the sheep,
Knots them and sinks, eyes blue as a moor loch.
There are children in gales;
I had five hands to guide me home, stories
Big as salmon. A goat, grandfather stern,
Stutters over the cabbages, ripe for the picking.

I hunch under the lintel
And thud the long exile from my boots.

Kenneth Steven

Invitation

We're splashing in the river on this sunny summer's day
With shoals of little fishes – you can watch them dart away,
Zig-zagging through the water till they disappear from view.
I wish that you could see them, Grandad. Won't you paddle, too?

The river bed is shining gold, with sparkling speckled stones –
Roll up your trousers quickly; we don't want to hear your groans.
Let little Matthew show you how he's nearly learned to swim.
He's waving to you, Grandad. Won't you come and look at him?

The water feels so lovely as it ripples round our feet;
If only you would join us it would make our day complete.
We want to go in deeper, to the shadow of the trees,
We promise we'll look after you, so come in, Grandad, please.

Tessa-Jo Stone

from the Manse Window

From A Distance

WHO doesn't love a perfect summer's evening? The sort of evening when the warmth of the day lingers on, the scents of the garden intensify and it's still possible to sit outside in perfect ease – preferably sharing a glass of something cold in pleasant company!

A few days ago I was doing just that with my good neighbours, Joe and Carol, when a sudden sound made us look up.

It was the muffled roar of a propane burner, and it came from a hot-air balloon that was drifting, otherwise silently, high above our heads in the cloudless sky.

For a moment I think that each one of us rather envied those passengers in the wicker basket suspended beneath the scarlet-striped envelope, looking down upon the dreaming countryside.

A few years ago, I myself had been lucky enough to enjoy just such an experience, which, despite my initial nerves, turned into a wonderful and memorable occasion.

But for Joe the sight prompted an entirely different train of thought.

As long as I've known him, he's been a keen amateur archaeologist, so neither Carol nor I were too surprised by his next remark.

"Did you know," he asked me, "that the first aerial archaeology was carried out with the aid a hot-air balloon?"

I did not, so he continued to enlighten me.

"It was in 1906, and was carried out by a Lieutenant Philip Sharpe of the Royal Engineers Balloon Section.

"The balloon was actually tethered, but it did allow him to ascend high enough to take three photographs of Stonehenge.

"And if anyone at the time had thought the venture foolish, they were soon proved wrong, for the photos turned out to be really informative.

"I suppose that nowadays, especially with the use of camera drones, we take the

by Maggie Ingall

58

use of aerial information for granted, but at the time it was revolutionary.

"After being used to examining things on hands and knees, it must have come as quite a shock to discover you might find out even more by looking from further away!"

Carol smiled.

"And did you know, Joe, you've just put me in mind of one of my favourite songs. That one called 'From a Distance'.

"It was written by an American songwriter called Julie Gold. Believe it or not, at first she had quite a job to find anyone to record it, but eventually Nanci Griffith put it on an album – and from there it took off.

"Do you know it?" She looked at me.

I did, indeed, for it's one that I, too, like very much.

I quoted one of the lines: "From a distance there is harmony, and it echoes through the land . . ."

For a moment we sat in thought, gazing at the drifting balloon.

"Well, I like to believe that the world is indeed becoming more harmonious," Joe said, "even if we aren't achieving it as quickly as we could or should.

"But I do think that getting a bit of perspective on things can help – whether it's assisting us to unravel the secrets of the past, or avoid the possible pitfalls of the future."

"And not forgetting," I added, "it can also help us cope with everyday life right now.

"After all, a bit of perspective can help with all sorts of things."

"I'm sure that's true," Carol agreed. "I do remember that when I was teaching I often found my pupils to be so focused upon their own particular worries that it made it very difficult for them to stand back and see things in proper proportion. That often made them feel very alone."

"Was there any way to help?" I wondered, thinking far back to my own adolescence, with all its preoccupations and uncertainties.

She looked more cheerful.

"Well, whenever I could, I found the most useful thing was to ask them if they would kindly support a fellow student.

"Not only did it help them feel valued, it nearly always enabled them to start talking more openly and easily about all sorts of things – which in turn helped them to realise their own concerns were rarely unique."

Another gentle hiss of gas made us glance up again. The balloon was further away now, but it was still the only sound to disturb the quiet evening.

The interruption gave me the chance to reflect upon an experience of my own, several years ago.

While living in another town, I once had a neighbour who seemed very different in attitude from my good friends Carol and Joe.

She was a newcomer to the neighbourhood, and initially appeared to be most stand-offish, ignoring the cheerful greetings of myself and others, and never willing to pause for a chat.

Only later did I learn from a random remark from a mutual acquaintance that the newcomer suffered from hearing loss.

She had spent her first few weeks in the area waiting for her new hearing aids, which had been mistakenly delivered to her old address.

Eventually she and I became good friends, but it certainly taught me a lesson, and I resolved in future that, before jumping to conclusions, I might spend a moment wondering if there was a wider picture of which I was unaware!

Ever the archaeologist, Joe continued on his own theme.

"I wonder how often the people of past times got too close to their own problems to see clearer solutions.

"I suspect it was just as frequently as we do! Ah, well – digging and delving can inform us of a great many things, but probably not that."

"Well, never mind," Carol said stoutly. "Whatever the answer, it doesn't mean that we can't try. I shall do my best, anyway."

And as we watched the balloon finally drift out of sight, I, for one, resolved to do exactly the same. ■

Nature's Calendar For *Summer*

In Season: New Potatoes

New potatoes are potatoes picked at an early stage of growth. They are sweeter than regular potatoes, and contain vitamin B1 and folic acid, as well as plenty of carbohydrates to keep you going as the days get longer!

On The Farm: Sheep Shearing

Because sheep don't shed their coats like other animals, they need sheared for summer. It is a costly job for farmers, with labour cost often being more than the value of the wool. In recent years, farmers have seen the wool have more value as fertiliser than as a material.

National Insect Week

The last week of June is earmarked for celebrating insects, a vital part of the ecosystem. Insect numbers have dropped alarmingly over the last few decades. Leaving part of your garden to go wild helps, providing breeding grounds and food, which in turn helps birds, bats and other creatures that depend on them.

Baby Deer

Wildlife charities are at pains to stress that fawns should not be rescued, even if they appear injured or abandoned. They are often left while the mother is away looking for food, and if you come across one the advice is to walk away and leave it in peace. Chances are the mother is closer than you think.

Tree Life: Green Leaves

Leaves are solar panels for trees, absorbing light for photosynthesis. Pine tree needles do the same, but are better for adverse environments like wind, snow and ice, and are better at retaining water. Because they don't drop, they work all year round.

In Season: Spring Greens

Spring greens are cabbages caught early before the thick centre develops. Early leaves aren't as potent in flavour or as tough, so can be eaten cooked or raw. The deep green colour hints at the wealth of nutrients inside, which help against a number of conditions, including heart disease and strokes, as well as having anti-inflammatory properties.

My Robin

I have a brand-new friend
Who lives high up in a tree,
And when I'm busy weeding
He comes right up close to me.
With his chubby little body
And his beady, darting eyes,
He keeps one eye on the worms
And the other on the skies.
And when a juicy, little morsel
Comes slithering on its way,
He grabs it, then he's off
Until it's next week's weeding day.

Lily Christie

The Cliff Path

High up it feels quite blustery,
Although the sun is bright,
And pleasure boats seem tiny
When viewed from this great height.
Against the rocks, sea holly
Shines blue against the grey,
And golden gorse and sea thrift
All add to the display.
When standing on a cliff top,
Behind, the rolling moors,
And gazing round at land and sea
The world seems truly yours!

Eileen Hay

Sunny Holidays

Satchel dumped in corner,
Along with any woes;
Skirt and blouse abandoned,
Replaced by outdoor clothes.

Running to the playing field,
Swinging on the swings
And pretending to be famous,
Like stars or queens and kings.

Rounders, tag and tennis
Created such a noise,
With strategy – plus cheating –
Until we beat the boys!

Climbing through the hedgerows
We'd wander off quite far,
But scurry back at teatime,
Taking tadpoles home in jars.

Grace Gant

The Paraglider

On earth, the rig seems clumsy,
A web of line and strap.
He buckles up the harness;
The foil begins to flap.
The wind blows strong and steady;
He starts the run downhill;
The canopy's inflating –
He feels the lift, the thrill.
And now he's soaring upwards,
Swung high on thermal breeze,
As graceful as a swallow
That skims the fields and trees.
Too soon the earth will claim him,
Too soon the grass will rise,
But just for now, in wonder,
On silken wing, he flies!

Maggie Ingall

A Delicate Rose

To think of summer is to think of a rose
And its delicate, scented mist,
Its gentle fragrance surrounding us,
As though the air has been kissed.
Its velvet petals blushing and blooming,
Its colours so vivid and bright,
With subtle turns it faces the sun
To bathe in warmth and light.
So majestic in the garden,
I could stare at a rose for hours –
There is no doubt at all;
She is the queen of all the flowers.

Lily Christie

Digging Potatoes

At first there is nothing. The wet spade
Levers up a few shards of pottery,
A dangling rage of earthworms –
But nothing else. Then I sink deeper
And suddenly the plant struggles up,
Heavy, like waterlogged seaweed on to a boat,
With misshapen things the colour of skin
Cheeked with pink. I drum them into a bucket
And wonder at a strange earth
That comes up with such lumps to fill our hunger.

Kenneth Steven

Where To Go

I'm ready for my holiday
And need to find somewhere to stay.
The city and bright lights, maybe?
So much to do, so much to see.

With nightclubs, restaurants and bars
And musicals with superstars,
And buskers entertaining queues,
There's so much on it's hard to choose.

However . . .

Leaving all these things behind me –
Hidden where no-one can find me
In some sleepy country hollow
With a wealth of tracks to follow

Makes the very thought delightful;
City life can be quite frightful.
Countryside receives my backing.
It's no contest. Let's get packing!

Dennis W. Turner

The Wedding At Cana

iStock.

RECENTLY I was preparing a children's talk about the wedding that Jesus attended at Cana. You may remember the story.

Like all weddings, it was no doubt a very happy occasion, with a beautiful bride and a handsome, doting bridegroom, proud parents and guests in their finery, all set to enjoy a wonderful celebration.

But there was a hiccup! At the reception, the wine ran out. There was nothing left to drink, and I imagine the night was still young.

Having done the catering for my own daughter's wedding some years ago, I could empathise with the poor bridegroom's father in this story.

As our wedding guests were called out from tables to go for their food, I remember keeping a watchful eye on the buffet table and becoming rather concerned when I saw the heaped platefuls of the eager young people!

Would the beef, salmon and the salads run out? Would there be enough sausages for the children?

And what about the desserts?

I suppose if this were happening today, I would have had the extra concerns of providing fat-free, gluten-free and vegan options!

On our happy occasion I needn't have worried. As always, I had made way too much, all to be enjoyed with friends in the days that followed.

Jesus and his family were among the guests at the wedding in Cana.

He may have noticed the predicament when the wine ran out, but it seems he didn't jump in to fix it.

His mother, Mary, would have discerned that something was up.

She obviously was aware of the servants whispering and the anxious faces of the hosts.

She must have known that Jesus could do something to help because she approached him with the words, "They have no wine left."

"You must not tell me what to do," Jesus replied.

We may think this a rather rude response of Jesus to his

By Janice Ross

mother. Perhaps the translation doesn't quite grasp the manner and tone in which this reply was given, as we read elsewhere that Jesus was an obedient and respectful son.

However, Jesus appreciated that, no matter the need or the person asking him for help, he could do nothing unless his father permitted him.

There was a time for miracles and acts of power and authority, but these were all in his father's hand and would only be ordained by him.

On this occasion, Jesus obviously heard his father give him permission to perform a miracle – to everyone's relief.

Wine is, of course, a mixture of fruit, alcohol, sugars and other organic molecules.

In Jesus's time, this was made very much in the way we might visualise.

Grapes were harvested in the fields and brought to nearby wine presses made of stone.

Workers stamped and trod on the grapes until the juice flowed into vats.

After passing through rough filters of twigs, the wine was collected and kept in the cool underground to prevent evaporation and to slow down the fermentation process.

As clean water was not always available in this warm, dry land, wine was a common drink, enjoyed daily at mealtimes and shared with friends.

Connoisseurs will inform us that it is not only the flavour of the wine, but also its colour, feel and smell that makes for a good product.

There can be no doubt that water and wine are not the same!

In changing water into wine, Jesus changed one substance into a completely different substance.

Jesus was doing more than simply helping out an embarrassed father here.

It is estimated that this miracle produced about 120 gallons of wine – the equivalent of about 700 bottles of the finest.

What an extravagant answer to a need! And what a wedding party that must have been!

This miracle, like those to follow, revealed much about God to Jesus's followers and taught them much deeper truths.

He was a God who lavished his grace and kindness on people. He was a God of the impossible, a God who could do anything.

In the next chapter of John's gospel, Jesus is in Jerusalem and is visited one night by Nicodemus, who was a Pharisee and a prominent Jewish leader.

The Pharisees were a group that violently opposed Jesus, and no doubt Nicodemus was taking a great risk by seeking out Jesus's counsel.

We are told that he recognised Jesus as a teacher come from God.

We are not told why he sought out Jesus, or what his first question might have been. It was obvious, however, that Jesus knew his heart.

"You need to be born again," Jesus tells him. "You need a change of nature."

What a strange statement. I wonder if Nicodemus had heard about the wine, or even been at the wedding?

Did the memory of that occasion come back to his mind?

Just as water becoming wine seemed a natural impossibility, so these words about new birth were equally impossible.

Can you imagine Nicodemus's puzzled expression when he asks, "How can I go back into the womb and be born again?"

"You can't in the flesh," Jesus replied, "but this is possible by the spirit."

Think about it, Nicodemus. At the wedding in Cana, simply filtering and cleaning water, storing it underground for months, then adding a rich red food colouring, or even somehow giving it a perfume, could never have changed the water into wine.

Nicodemus learned an important truth through this encounter.

Just as water can never become wine, neither could his good works nor his best efforts be a suitable offering to God.

All the good practices of his flesh could never make him acceptable. He needed a new nature.

Only God can provide us with this new nature, and he is as eager to bless us with this provision as he was to bless needy guests with the choicest of wine. ■

Nature's Calendar For Summer

In Season: Greengages

Greengages are not the easiest fruit to grow in the UK, but are said to be tastier than plums when at their peak. They're native to the warmer climes of Armenia and Iran and were brought to the UK by Sir Thomas Gage.

On The Farm: Combine Harvesters

Combine harvesters work in fields late into the summer evenings. They're named for "combining" these four processes into one machine: reaping, threshing, gathering and winnowing.

World Water Week

This annual event invites delegates to come together to challenge the world's water problems. Over a billion people lack access to clean, fresh water, and nearly half the world's population will experience scarcity of water at some point due to climate change – whether natural or human-made.

Shrew Breeding

The humble water shrew finishes its breeding season at the end of summer. They live along the edges of clean, unpolluted water in the UK and there are estimated to be around three-quarters of a million. They are under threat from increased pollution in rivers, and are completely absent from Ireland and the Isle of Man.

Tree Life: Growing

Trees at the Equator reach maturity in as little as 10-20 years, while trees in the boreal forest of the far north can take over 100 years, due to a growing season as short as three months. The slowest growing tree in the world reportedly grew to only four inches after 150 years – a white cedar in Canada.

In Season: Sweetcorn

Sweetcorn, now available in supermarkets in its natural on-the-cob form, is actually full of useful phytochemicals and insoluble fibre that is good for your gut. A whole ear still contains less sugar than an apple or banana. It's also important not to confuse it with the different crop used to make high-fructose corn syrup, which is virtually inedible.

Nature's Company

The pathway leading
To the shore
Is fringed with campion,
Thrift and more.
Above us, sun
And cloudless sky,
With scattered seagulls
Floating by.

I love it here,
Where no man's hand
Has touched the sea
Or silver sand,
Where few explore
Its empty space,
Preferring some more
Crowded place.

It makes me glad
That we could find
A place to leave
All cares behind.
A paradise
Where we can be
At one in
Nature's company.

John Darley

People Of The Sea

Have you been where seals come dancing,
Bobbing, leaping by the shore?
Have you seen their dark eyes shining
From those inlets they explore?
Tales of myth and lore and legend,
Selkie – people of the sea –
From the western coast of Scotland,
The place they first made friends with me.

Across those wide and sunlit waters
I call with songs they love and know,
And soulful notes I play to charm them
With my fiddle and my bow.
Dreamy music, soft and haunting,
That speaks of visions wild and free;
"I am a man upon the land,
I am a selkie in the sea."

Dawn Lawrence

Somewhere

Rolling hillsides clad in pine trees,
Tiny village nestling near,
Set beside a shingle seashore,
Lapped by waters calm and clear.
Woodlands green are filled with birdsong,
Whitewashed houses snug below,
Painted boats within the harbour,
Safe from any storms that blow.
Did I dream this gentle haven?
Was this where I once did roam?
Real or myth, if I should find it,
Then at last I'll know I'm home.

Maggie Ingall

Autumn's Glory

It's like a magic trick each year,
The way green's made to disappear,
Replaced by copper, red and gold
As autumn's days start to unfold.

I never tire of seeing how
Every tree, on every bough,
Provides a vibrant free-for-all,
Before those leaves begin to fall.

I love this season, even though
What follows might bring frost and snow.
But while the days may soon be duller,
Nature fills it, now, with colour.

John Darley

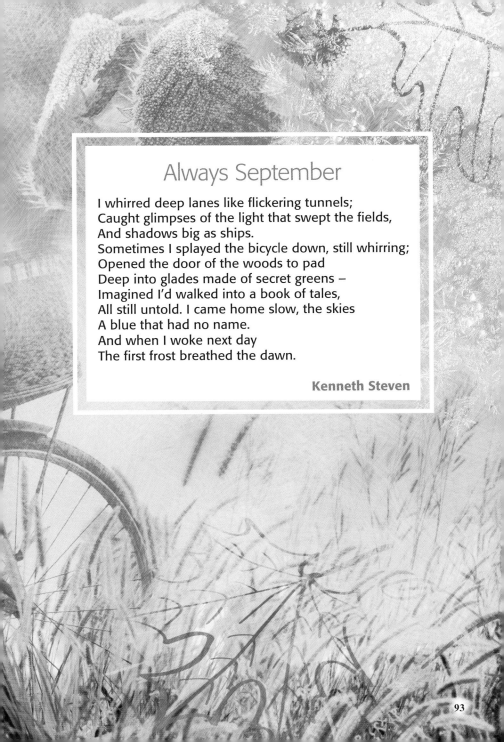

Always September

I whirred deep lanes like flickering tunnels;
Caught glimpses of the light that swept the fields,
And shadows big as ships.
Sometimes I splayed the bicycle down, still whirring;
Opened the door of the woods to pad
Deep into glades made of secret greens –
Imagined I'd walked into a book of tales,
All still untold. I came home slow, the skies
A blue that had no name.
And when I woke next day
The first frost breathed the dawn.

Kenneth Steven

The Artist
Known As A

My Alfie is an artist,
Unique at only two.
The kitchen wall's his canvas;
His medium is food.

He likes to use his fingers,
His palms or sometimes fists,
He smears it and he throws it –
Duck or take the risk.

Pasta sauce is favourite,
The colour and the goo,
And to add a pleasing texture
Veg gets thrown there, too.

He is an abstract artist,
At least that's what I think.
But once the muse has left him,
He goes for forty winks.

I wash his cartoon palette,
His tray and baby spoon,
Wipe his canvas nice and clean,
For the new piece coming soon.

Heather Walker

Come Back
Little Swallow

Come back, little swallow,
Please don't fly away.
Though the days they are
shortening,
We'd love for you to stay.
You're the emblem of summer,
You're a most welcome guest,
And you've worked really hard
To build up that sweet nest.
It's a long way back home,
Your wings will soon tire;
When the weather grows cold,
You can perch by our fire.
The autumn will pass and the
Winter soon follow,
Then spring's on its way,
So please stay, little swallow.

Dave Dutton

97

The Scarecrow

It's a funny old life being a scarecrow;
I just stand here quite still all the day,
As the bright golden corn grows around me,
And I scare all the bad birds away!
Are you thinking I look well and dandy,
In this jacket so smart and so fine?
It was once Sunday best for the farmer,
But I'm happy to say it's now mine!
Yes, I know that the trousers are baggy,
And they have the odd patch here and there,
But my straw fills them out really nicely,
And it matches the straw of my hair!
You may think that my life as a scarecrow
Means I don't know too much, but you're wrong –
'Cos I know all the bees by their buzzing
And I know all the birds by their song.
I can stand here in sunshine or showers,
And I'm happy as happy can be,
So what more can a scarecrow be asking?
I'm at one with all nature you see.

Eileen Hay

from the Manse Window

The Leaves That Are Green

iStock.

BEAUTIFUL melodies often carry sorrowful lyrics. Sweet harmonies can clothe bitter thoughts or a broken heart.

Take the 1966 song by Simon and Garfunkel, "The Leaves That Are Green".

While it sounds lovely, it's actually about the themes of time and change and loss.

A romance has budded and blossomed but is now fading, "and the leaves that are green turn to brown, and they wither with the wind, and they crumble in your hand . . ."

The image of autumn here suggests the best is past, time is bringing a season of decline and regret.

Leaves are changing colour and will soon fall like the accelerating shadows of evening.

We all naturally love the budding new life of spring as the days get warmer, but I actually like autumn!

I'd rather have the unexpected bonus of a calm day in October than the disappointment of a wet day in July!

I love how even though summer is officially over and we're heading inevitably towards winter, the gardens and parks are clothed in majestic splendour!

The colours of the trees are sublime and I confess a childlike pleasure in kicking our way through a crisp carpet of leaves.

As another song puts it, "We walk in fields of gold."

Romantic poet John Keats died tragically young, but not before penning the famous words recited still in many school classrooms:

Season of mists and mellow fruitfulness,

Close bosom friend of the maturing sun;

Conspiring with him how to load and bless

With fruit the vines that round the thatch-eves run;

To bend with apples the moss'd cottage-trees,

And fill all fruit with ripeness to the core;

To swell the gourd, and plump the hazel shells

With a sweet kernel, to set

▶

By Rev. Andrew Watson

> *budding more . . .*

In contrast to Simon and Garfunkel's song, Keats sees autumn as a culmination, a crowning of the year with the fullness of the harvest and ripening of fruit.

Yes, spring emerges from winter with cheery "songs" of bright hope, but autumn, "thou hast thy music too" the poet insists, speaking of a countryside chorus of insects, birds and sheep.

Autumn has its own unique beauty and even through experiences of sad loss we can discover new richness and the fruit of maturity.

If we take the four seasons as a picture of life with spring as youth and summer as the blossoming of early adulthood, then autumn should be the season to enjoy a harvest of decisions sown in the wisdom we have acquired with the years.

We're familiar with the saying "older and wiser".

If we're willing to learn, experience can help us avoid repeating earlier mistakes and do things better!

Jesus spoke of God like a skilled horticulturist pruning back a vine to make it more fruitful.

Gardeners are familiar with the concept. In typically dramatic style Christ declared, "Unless a kernel of wheat falls to the ground and dies, it remains only a single seed.

"But if it dies, it produces many seeds."

At the heart of Christianity is this irony, that it's by our lord's suffering and death, his "autumn and winter" as it were, that new and everlasting life is multiplied and made available to the world.

The apostle Paul would later write of the "fruit" blossoming from a life led and enriched by the holy spirit Jesus gives, wonderful qualities like love, joy, peace, patience, kindness, goodness, gentleness, faithfulness and self-control.

Yes, please!

James takes a slightly different angle, promising, "Peacemakers who sow in peace raise a harvest of righteousness."

The writer of Hebrews revisits the idea of pruning, that God as a loving father on occasions trains and where necessary corrects his children, which can seem unpleasant but in time "produces a harvest of righteousness and peace."

His plans for us are good.

So while none of us would go looking for difficult or painful circumstances they can bring opportunities to grow and blossom in fresh ways.

We receive help from beyond ourselves. We find resilience and courage we didn't know we had.

Surviving redundancy or a family tragedy, having to overcome fear to learn new skills, choosing to avoid the cancer of resentment, being willing to practise kindness and compassion throughout . . .

These are not easy or pleasant lessons, but they can bring reward to those who, with determination, make up our mind to "trust in the lord and do good."

And as often happens, blessing overflows to touch others as people mature inwardly and learn new ways to show love.

It's not that complicated. Solitude can give us empathy for neighbours facing isolation.

We might become more considerate and imaginative. A call, a message or small gift perhaps?

A little kindness can mean so much.

Perhaps we find that simply sharing a little of our story honestly encourages someone else to keep going under pressure.

Perhaps our enthusiasm for coming to church and our daily prayers could encourage someone else to explore faith.

Perhaps our obedience in following our master's example of generous compassion for the poor and in need could literally save a life somewhere in the world, or inspire a little more respect among neighbours from differing backgrounds.

All good results. Fruit pleasing to God.

The leaves that are green turn to brown. But many of them turn gold.

Life will have days of sadness and loss.

But have you ever noticed how in autumn people chop wood for winter and plant bulbs for the resurrection that comes with spring? People practise faith without even knowing it!

Christians trust in Jesus and his promises that those who follow him through all seasons will not only grow in fruitful living presently, but enjoy wholeness of life with him eternally! ■

Nature's Calendar For *Autumn*

National Organic Month

September is National Organic Month, raising awareness of organic produce. Produced to strict standards, organic food can be better for you. Research showed organic apples contained more beneficial bacteria than a conventional apple, aiding the health of your gut.

In Season: Mangetout

This variety of peas are picked well before the peas inside develop, and eaten along with the pod. Best eaten when as crisp and vivid green as possible, they're known as snow peas in the US. Mangetout help pull nitrogen in the atmosphere into the ground around them, benefiting plants growing nearby.

Fox Fights

Fox families might be heard or even seen fighting. As autumn rolls on, the family unit breaks up and the young will usually strike out on their own. Before they part ways, cubs are often fighting amongst themselves for food – or sometimes with their own parents, once they're on the cusp of complete self-sufficiency.

Shutterstock.

In Season: Wild Mushrooms

In some parts of Italy, you can have any wild mushrooms you pick checked for free, to ensure they're edible. Courses on picking wild mushrooms are widely available, and are a great way to enjoy nature's autumnal harvest with expert supervision!

On The Farm: Ploughing

Ploughing matches are commonly held through the autumn months, where farmers are judged for their straight lines and decent shape of the furrows. Often there are classes for both tractor-drawn ploughs and for horse-drawn.

Evidence of using ploughs to grow crops exists as far back as 2000 BC in ancient Egypt.

Tree Life: Fruit

The harvest of fruit trees is in full swing. Removing the fruit is also good for the tree. Heading into the colder months, picking the fruit – even inedible ones – is part of preparing them for the winter. Pruning, removing fallen leaves and inspecting for pests are all important to their health during their dormant months and for their revival. Rotten fruits at the base may attract bugs.

Harvest Time

The summer now has slipped away
And harvest time is here.
A time for giving heartfelt thanks
As many gifts appear.

A season filled with bounty,
Of flowers, fruit and grain,
And so much Mother Nature gives
Produced by sun and rain.

And so give thanks with gratefulness,
Rejoice with song and rhyme,
And share the harvest with the world,
Give thanks at harvest time!

Iris Hesselden

Family Tree

My father made a mission
To trace our family tree,
With patient care and time to spare,
He did so reverently.
And so we have amassed a trove
Of details of our past,
Our lineage surprised us all;
Sometimes we were aghast.
Links to homes of grandeur,
An author lurked there, too,
Amazing that such secrets
Were hidden from our view.
And Dad put all that legwork in,
With links he carefully found,
Until the jigsaw formed and grew,
In volumes leather bound.
And now he's passed the records on,
Entrusting them to me,
My father's hard-won legacy,
Our treasured family tree.

Judy Jarvie

Family Tree

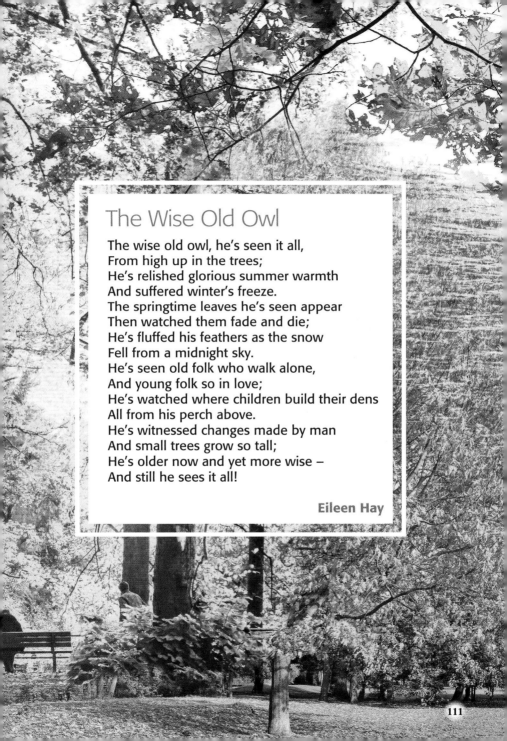

The Wise Old Owl

The wise old owl, he's seen it all,
From high up in the trees;
He's relished glorious summer warmth
And suffered winter's freeze.
The springtime leaves he's seen appear
Then watched them fade and die;
He's fluffed his feathers as the snow
Fell from a midnight sky.
He's seen old folk who walk alone,
And young folk so in love;
He's watched where children build their dens
All from his perch above.
He's witnessed changes made by man
And small trees grow so tall;
He's older now and yet more wise –
And still he sees it all!

Eileen Hay

Shining Through

There's a shiver in the wheat fields,
A brush upon the breeze,
The trees are uneasy
With trembling of the leaves.
There's a stirring of temper,
As nature has its way,
To strike at any moment,
To paint the scenery grey.
Now the roar of thunder,
The clap, bang and flash,
The fish go deeper diving,
To avoid the mighty crash.
Soon, all is calm again,
A fragrant earth once more,
A rainbow shining in the sky,
And the birds, in happiness, soar.

Dorothy McGregor

The Hallowe'ens Of Yesteryear

We wore bin bags, and old bed sheets
As costumes on the night,
Bought cheap, elasticated masks,
To give our friends a fright.

Our pumpkins were not works of art –
They just had funny faces.
We carried all our sweets and treats
In worn out pillow-cases.

We bobbed for apples every year,
Told old stories 'til ten –
This atmospheric, happy time
Was so much fun back then.

Michelle Illing

Bonfire Night

Fire light and bonfire bright!
Time to gather round.
We feel excitement in the air,
And magic to be found.
The fireworks are beautiful,
With stars of gold and white;
We wish that they would never stop,
And just go on all night!

So share the coffee and the tea,
Or toffee in a tin,
And who cares if the night is cold
When we are warm within.
We've found such joy and wonder,
Excitement and delight,
And we will all remember
The thrill of Bonfire Night!

Iris Hesselden

At Peace

A simple, granite gravestone
Shows where the warrior lies;
In silent peace he rests now,
Beneath these safer skies.
No more will sounds of battle
Impel him into life,
This hallowed earthly setting
Has released him from such strife.

There comes a time when all things
pass,
For those who once knew fame,
When, only in the history books,
Will they recall his name.
But what he did is evident,
In the lives we live today,
By fighting for our freedom,
With a price we can't repay.

John Darley

Home Is Where The Heart Goes

HOME. What does that word mean to you?

For me, it was an end-terrace house on a hill overlooking a seaside town.

There were gaps in the terracing because the hillside had been mined and certain areas were likely to sink if they were built on.

Revisiting recently, I appreciated the view out over the sea. Back then, I was considerably shorter and didn't even know we had a view.

Looking at my old home from across the road, for the first time in 50-something years, I recognised it – but there was no emotional connection.

So, trying not to look too suspicious, I sat down on the kerb.

That made me about the same height I was when I was five.

My heart remembered and reached out to it.

We had been poor back then – but we children never knew it! All we knew was love, and belonging.

My mother, being a soppy type, kept various things from back then, amongst which was a drawing I did of family and home when I was about three.

For some reason we are all wearing wellington boots and we all have prominent belly buttons. But the house . . .

It's a square, with a triangular roof, four windows, a door in the middle, and a chimney with a spiral of smoke coming from it. There were no neighbours.

The door, in reality, was in a different position, the windows were different . . . but I was a child. How much accuracy could be expected?

My own daughter, when she was about the same age, drew a similar house, complete with smoking chimney.

But she had never lived in a house with a chimney – all her homes had central heating.

Apparently, it's a recognised phenomenon. Children will draw their house, their home, in the same way, no matter if they live in a tower block or a bungalow.

The image of home is a ▶

iStock.

By David McLaughlan

120

▶ strong one and it is with us from a very early age.

Children who might never have known a real home because of war or natural disaster find themselves longing for aspects of home the rest of us take for granted – like a bed, like a door to close, like a garden outside.

All of this came to mind as I walked through a country park, kicking up crisp brown leaves.

The park rangers run activities for children throughout the year and one of them is den-building. The dens tend to be low-tech affairs, using broken branches, with a lean-to being the upper level of sophistication.

This was something else.

The grass had been blown flat by winds and rain, the trees were bare, and autumn had been around long enough for several branches to have dried and fallen to the ground.

Someone, or a group of someones, had gathered up some longer branches and then, with the help of some tatty old nylon rope, fixed them to the trees.

Ingeniously, they seemed to have recreated that childhood archetype of a house.

Horizontal branches played the tops and bottoms of the four walls (in a rough square). Branches stuck on to the ground framed a doorway, and square window-frames were hung on rope between the doorway and the corner trees.

They had even attempted the triangular roof, but it had collapsed before I arrived. A soggy cardboard box lay among the "ruins". Had this been their chimney, I wondered?

As there were no chairs inside, let alone a kettle or a TV, I kept walking, smiling and humming to myself.

"Be it ever so humble, there's no place like home."

I appreciated my own humble abode all the more when I got there.

Perhaps not surprisingly, the concept of "home" is an essential part of what it means to be human.

It's where we come from, where we were cared for when we couldn't care for ourselves, where we rest at the end of each day.

It should, in an ideal world, be where we are always welcome. And it's where we retire to when all our earthly resources are coming to an end.

As human beings, we don't always have all of that all the time, but the notion of it, the need for it, runs deep within us.

When we don't have it, we really feel the lack.

Which is why it strikes such a jarring note when Jesus, in the Book of Luke, says, "Foxes have dens and birds have nests but the son of man has no place to lay his head."

Isn't he, of all people, supposed to understand what's important to us? He was born in Bethlehem and raised in Nazareth, so why does he claim to have no home?

A clue might be found in one of the few times he talks about what happens after this life.

He says, "In my father's house there are many mansions; if it were not so, I would have told you. I go to prepare a place for you."

So, in what might be his clearest description of heaven, he talks of homes; of many homes within a larger heavenly home.

Having come from such a wonderful place, perhaps we shouldn't be surprised that he didn't concern himself with ideas of a home in this world.

And perhaps it helps explain why the notion of, and the need for, home runs so deep within us. Because it's where we belong, and where we are heading.

Jesus also promised the thief on the cross that, in the next life, he would be with Jesus in paradise. Does that sound dramatically different from "many mansions"?

Well, I look back to my own first home where we had nothing but, in my innocence, because we had each other and we had a home of our own, I thought we had everything.

I can't imagine paradise being much more wonderful than that. ■

Nature's Calendar For *Autumn*

Roosting Bats

Bats may roost in a number of places during the year, but they really pick their spot for their winter hibernation. Often they move to caves underground.

Nobody knows where all the pipistrelles go, though – nobody's found enough winter roosts to account for them all!

In Season: Brussels Sprouts

Just 80 g of sprouts contain more Vitamin C than an orange! This traditional festive veg benefits from the first frost to add flavour, and it is named after the Belgian city around which it was a popular crop. It's also one of the few vegetables to contain protein, in addition to other nutrients.

Tree Life: Leaf Fall

The trees' loss is the planet's gain. Leaf fall adds nutrients to the earth's soil – as well as providing winter cover for important insect and animals species. Shredded leaves can be added to compost or soil to give a boost to anything you're hoping to grow come the new year, so don't burn them or throw them away.

Shutterstock.

In Season: Pumpkins

Pumpkins need to be picked before the first frost, and require fairly warm temperatures during the summer to be at their best. If you can grow them, they're not just good for carving – pumpkin soup is delicious and can be served within the hollowed-out pumpkin.

You can also wash, dry, roast and season the seeds for a tasty snack.

On The Farm: Hedgecutting

With birds now having left their nests, farmers turn their attention to hedges. Some hedgerows are protected by law, and trimming during nesting season is an offence. Hedgerows provide food and shelter for wildlife, and work as safe "highways" for some species to move around in.

World Town Planning Day

World Town Planning Day takes place on November 8 every year. It's about drawing attention to the importance of building liveable communities. We still have a lot to learn about building new homes and redeveloping areas with an accent on green spaces, community facilities and other human and natural needs.

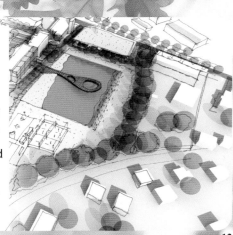

Guiding Light

I watch the water with a roving eye,
While terns and gulls go screeching by.
The breeze they ride is kind today –
If only it would stay that way,
For oftentimes the storm winds blow,
Whipping waves up far below
'Til they begin to rage and roar,
And that's when sailors look to shore,
Seeking guidance from the light,
Atop my stripes of red and white.
Two hundred years I've stood before –
Will I survive two hundred more?

Laura Tapper

Blown Away

I would like to talk umbrellas,
Or brollies, just for short.
They're a science and a bother –
At least the legion I have bought.
As soon as I walk out the door,
Into the gusty rain,
They become inside-out parachutes,
As I struggle there, in vain.
With monsoons ever daily,
I fled to the shop's first floor,
Picked the nearest on the stand,
A strong one, costing more.
This one, beautiful and see-through,
With flowers, the best one yet,
And when the rain is pouring
I'm so happy that we met.

Dorothy McGregor

Goodbye To The Season

Now the sun has set on autumn,
Leaves blanket everything,
The trees will rest in tandem;
They'll wake again in spring.

Geese take flight in numbers,
A true sight to behold,
While hedgehogs turn to slumber,
Joined by dormice, bees and toads.

We gather close together
And settle warm inside.
No need to check the weather –
We've no plans to go outside.

In the mornings there are hints
Of winter's bright reveal;
A chilly draught, a frosted glint,
Through darker nights it steals.

Light a candle, pull the curtains,
Gather comforts close to hand.
As autumn fades we can be certain –
This winter will be grand.

Thelma Fairweather

Fire and Frost

A winter dawn with blazing sky
Alights like celestial fire,
And in the leafless trees the birds
Tune up their morning choir.
The frosted shrubs and frozen grass
Reflect the colours from on high,
So they, too, glow a sparkling red,
Competing with the glorious sky.
It looks surreal, this fiery scene,
A shining moment caught in time;
Such icy beauty feeds the soul –
Yes, nature's palette is sublime!

Eileen Hay

My Last Winter

I remember how the village was
Wrapped in snow so deep your legs sank.
Flakes as big as a cat's pads
Batting at windows till they disappeared.

Going out by night you felt you'd lost your way;
Houses up to their eyes in fleece, roofs under siege.
Pieces of stars like broken glass striking their fires,
And a gold nugget of moon floating in dark water.

It was so cold your chest burst into flames;
The air was blue and little bits of frost
Clung to its tongue. Along the rim of your mouth
White icing smiled.

That was the winter I went through the forest
Up to my waist in a white sea, arms splashing,
Till on a clearing's edge I saw the Northern Lights,
Like strange sledges with horses of silver and red.

Kenneth Steven

Happy Families

I've never been one for those card games,
Suggested when families meet;
I dream up excuses – "I'll make us a drink" –
Or wash up, or make something to eat.

"You all carry on there without me,
You don't want me spoiling your fun;
You've quite enough players already –
I could just catch the post, if I run."

Then along came a three-year-old grandchild,
With over-sized cards in small hands
And a wish to play "Happily Families",
And I say, "Of course! That sounds grand."

The family gasped in amazement;
"Well, this is a first!" they agree,
But a change in routine brings a problem –
"Who'll now make the coffee and tea?"

These days I'm a permanent fixture
At the card table, straight after dinner,
And my ample reward, the best thing in the world,
Is that grin when she shouts, "I'm the winner!"

Chris Young

Festive Display

Resplendent in the window,
Decked out in twinkling lights,
To share the hope of Christmas,
These dark December nights,
With any who are weary
Or weighted down with care.
Bless you, dearest neighbour,
For placing your tree there.

Laura Tapper

Magic Tree

"No tree this year." Mother sighed.
"Money's short, I fear."
Oh, I just would not be consoled,
And shed a fretful tear.

But my brothers and my sister said,
"We'l make a magic tree,
Better than a real one.
Just you wait and see."

They gathered string and paper,
Paint and wire and wood.
Worked so well together,
Like something understood.

I watched in silent wonder,
As it grew so fine and tall,
Its shades of green were fabulous,
Its magic touched us all.

They held me high to place the star,
Its light is still guiding me,
Down all the years it shines with
love
From our wondrous magic tree.

Kate Bradbury

from the Manse Window

Lessons From The Snow

IN the words of the seasonal song, "I'm dreaming of a white Christmas". But often we don't get one!

Depending on where we live, we find that we can escape heavy snowfalls in December and the chaos they bring in their train.

Weather conditions at the end of the year and into the next one can admittedly be seasonally cold and frosty, but nevertheless quite favourable.

Sometimes, of course, the snow waits to fall in the early months of the new year, and it's then that we have to cope with all the problems it brings.

From a church minister's point of view, snow is always problematic.

If I decided to prepare a story about snow or choose a hymn about it following a midweek snowfall, as sure as fate, by the time Sunday came round, it would have melted!

However, I do remember, one snowy Sunday morning, getting it just right.

The snow was still thick on the ground as the faithful people trudged through it and made their way to the Sunday service.

I took the opportunity to speak to the congregation on some words recorded in the book of Isaiah, words singularly appropriate in which the prophet spoke of the "treasures of the snow".

I reminded my congregation about how powerful a tiny snowflake can be when it gets together with billions of others.

You can catch a snowflake in your hand and dissolve it in seconds, but you couldn't do that if billions of snowflakes suddenly fell on top of you!

But I also reminded them of how beautiful the snow can look as it blankets the countryside, like a picture postcard.

It can make black rooftops white and even make piles of rubbish gleam.

"The manse garden never looks nicer than when it is covered in snow," I assured my congregation.

▶

iStock

By Rev. Ian W.F. Hamilton

The point which I went on to make, of course, was that when we look out on our lives we can see so many dull, black spots, we can see so many "rubbishy" things that have littered our lives, but then we remember that God's forgiveness is like a beautiful blanket of snow.

It comes down from heaven and covers all that's black and ugly in our lives and transforms these things into something lovely.

As Isaiah said on another occasion, 'Tho' your sins be as scarlet, they shall be white as snow."

For the children, snow time is fun time as they engage in sledging, snowman-building and no doubt snowball fights!

However, for the young and the not so young, snow brings with it its frustrations and problems.

Especially so on our roads; snow often causes absolute chaos, as I well remember, having had to negotiate the main highway from the central belt of Scotland through the notorious Drumochter Pass, via Aviemore, to my home in Nairn on the Moray coast.

On countless occasions I had to drive carefully behind snowploughs as they tried relentlessly to clear a pathway for northbound traffic on the great north road in order to keep it open.

The snowploughs are absolutely essential because when the snow has fallen so heavily, the roads and surrounding area become a big white carpet.

Not only does the white line down the centre of the road become invisible, it's also difficult to tell where the road ends and the ditch begins.

It's so hard to keep to the road in the slush and snow. You only need to go a few feet off track and you'll come to an untimely halt!

So if a necessary journey has to be made in heavy snowy conditions perhaps there are two ways in which we can try to keep to the road.

The first, in the absence of a snowplough, is to follow the tracks of a car which recently went along the road before you. Following established tracks is a way of helping you to reach your destination.

But what if you are the first person to use the particular road since the snow has so heavily fallen?

Well, a second method you could adopt – especially on a quiet country road – is to keep glancing up at the telegraph poles which usually run along the roadside, constantly and carefully judging your distance from them.

Of course, living our lives is like travelling along a road.

Normally the going isn't too bad, and the difference between the things that are right and the things that are wrong is patently obvious.

But on occasions the road can be very hard to follow. When this happens, again there are two ways in which we can keep going, and keep going in the right direction.

Firstly, we can follow the tracks of the people in front of us. Christian folks in every age have given us an example to follow, and if we try hard to follow in their footsteps we shouldn't go too far off course.

The second thing we can do, metaphorically speaking, is to keep glancing upwards, not to telegraph poles, but to God.

If we take our bearings and directions from him and his teachings in the Bible, and if we go the way in which God has clearly shown us to go, we will surely and safely reach our destination.

I'm reminded of some words from the lovely children's hymn we often sang in church.

"And if I try to follow his footsteps here below, he never will forsake me, because he loves me so."

Yes, a heavy snowfall in winter most certainly showers us with a catalogue of lessons.

It reminds us that God can cover our inadequate lives with a blanket of forgiveness, that a good strategy is to follow Christian souls who have trod the path of life before us.

And not least it assures us that if we look up to God our father in heaven and take our bearings from him, we will surely be given the sure and safe direction in which to travel on our onward journey through life.

So if you are "dreaming of a white Christmas", think on these things! ■

Shutterstock.

Nature's Calendar For *Winter*

Wader Birds

It's a special time of year to catch sight of wading birds. The birds – from Canada, Norway and Siberia – head to our climes for winter, settling into estuaries and tidal basins, where there's plenty food to go round.

The Wash, between Lincolnshire and Norfolk, houses half a million of them on its own.

In Season: Cranberries

This hardy, tart fruit is harvested in a most unusual way in the US. The fields it grows in are frequently flooded with about a foot of water to protect the plants from frost, but it's also done when they're ready to pick. The ripe fruits float up and are corralled together before getting sucked up by a pipe and washed for sale.

Houseplant Week UK

Every second week in January, the UK celebrates Houseplant Week! Houseplants not only look and smell nice, but they bring some of the mental health benefits of the great outdoors into our homes. Whether appreciating their appearance, or enjoying tending to them, studies back up the idea that they can make you happier.

In Season: Onions

The humble onion is a primary ingredient in cuisine around the world. It's important to remember that though they should be stored in similar conditions to potatoes, they shouldn't be kept together.

The potatoes will spoil quickly, absorbing the moisture and ethylene gas from the onions.

Tree Life: Evergreens

Evergreen trees provide a winter oasis for wildlife. The dense needle cover and close branches that help them survive in inhospitable climates provide shelter for birds, deer and rodents that aren't hibernating.

Owls can roost in them, deer will hide amongst them for shelter and squirrels are partial to the pine cones.

On The Farm: Get Indoors

As winter begins to bite, livestock will be moved indoors. It can be a dangerous job for farmers, herding so many beasts into a smaller space than they're used to. Good ventilation is key for ensuring herd health, too, as animals can be prone to pneumonia in cool, damp indoor environments.

A New Year Resolution

I'll make a resolution,
Just the one this year I think;
It should involve more exercise,
To keep me in the pink.

I might just take up yoga;
I am told it can be fun,
Whilst easing these stiff joints of mine
And helping me feel young.

Or power walking in the park,
That looks like serious stuff;
Or badminton or Zumba,
But they'd leave me out of puff.

Or maybe I should join a gym?
That could be quite effective.
Or I could take a weekly swim;
That might meet my objectives.

So many opportunities
At which to take a look;
But just for now, I'll curl up here,
And read my lovely book.

Chris Young

Nature's Paint

A blanket of peace begins to descend,
As gentle pure snowflakes swiftly transcend
The black naked trees from their stark winter dress
Into bridal white ladies decked out in their best.
The grass is bejewelled with diamonds so bright,
In a dazzling display in the winter sunlight,
Row upon row of iced cake smooth hills,
Lace covered windows with soft velvet sills.
Roads, tracks and pavements all blend into one,
As a sparkling, icy white carpet is spun.
The whole world is painted by nature's great gift,
Of transforming snowstorms and glistening drifts.
This was not the world when we all said goodnight,
What a wonderful, breathtaking, glorious sight.

Linda Brown

First Flurry

Hands stretching wide like starfish,
Eyes aglow with delight,
Giggles of joy at the dazzling display,
A new and magical sight.

Mouth wide open to taste one,
Cold and wet on his tongue ,
Little fist closing round a white flake,
Then open to find that it's gone!

Forehead creased in confusion –
"Daddy! Where did it go?
Will you help me, please Daddy, to
catch one?
I want to show Mummy my snow."

Kathryn Sennen

Auntie Lizzie

Auntie Lizzie
Is so busy,
Always on the go.
Mending, making,
Or bread-baking,
Rushing to and fro.

Now, Uncle Billy,
Willy-nilly,
Is more the ponderous type.
While Auntie flits,
He calmly sits,
Puffing on his pipe.

Auntie Lizzie,
Busy Lizzie,
Doesn't seem to care,
And Uncle Billy,
He's not silly,
He keeps mum in his chair.

John Darley

Dawn In The City

The city sleeps; just empty streets,
Some pigeons rooting round,
Enjoying their freedom from the cars
That normally abound.
The city's rhythms now are stilled,
Its massive heartbeat slowed;
The traffic lights go changing on
With little on the road.
A few weak rays of morning sun
Proclaim a brand-new day,
The eastern sky begins to glow
But street lamps still hold sway.
Then slowly darkness slips away,
Reality creeps in;
The city wakes, the hum of noise
Increases to a din.
And early workers stumble by,
With many a sigh and yawn;
The night's dark stillness is no more,
The magic dawn is gone.

Eileen Hay

The Biscuit Tin

I open the lid and peer inside, eager to dive in,
As my hand hovers expectantly above the biscuit tin.
Oh, crumbs! They're all delicious; there's just too much choice, it seems.
Should I pick the malted milk or the last two custard creams?
Garibaldi, jammy rings, cookies packed with chocolate chips,
Each a moment of pure pleasure as I lift it to my lips.
Pink wafers are the prettiest, brandy snaps have bite,
And you just can't beat a shortbread when you have an appetite.
But today the plain digestive is the only one for me,
Quickly turning soft and soggy, as I dunk it in my tea!

Vivien Brown

Pure Wonderland

No other spell spins like the snow,
Such pure and sheer delight.
The heavens have opened, we can't believe
This stunning and magical sight.
Icy flurries make a breathtaking gown,
Set with diamonds, winking in sun.
Pretty posies of snowdrops so delicate,
So precious in winter time spun.
The snow is lightly pirouetting down,
As the orchestra of silence plays on,
The fresh and freeze invigorates,
With stretches of white silvered frond.
The joy of the first snow, the whispers of chill,
The charm of all we survey,
Trace of the spider's exquisite webs,
So beautiful – a snow heaven day.

Dorothy McGregor

from the Manse Window

Healing
The Divide

PERHAPS I was just being fanciful, but everything else was coldly real.

I sat on a promenade bench with Andy, watching a watery, early evening sunset.

We spoke little enough to ask what needed to be asked and say what needed to be said.

He had spent the night before last walking the streets. The night before we met up, he had been too tired to walk any further and he fell asleep on the beach we were looking out over.

We lived very different lives, had very different expectations. But, sitting there together, I imagined I could feel the cold of the pointless streets.

I felt a little of what it must have been like to have no-one at all to turn to, and I thought I felt the salty sand in the crease of my cheek.

And I knew we both watched the sun sink beneath the horizon in awe.

I remember Andy when I think of how divided the world seems to

have become recently. And how it doesn't have to be.

Perhaps we aren't all that polarised, and it's just that online communications make it seem so. It is easy to argue with someone whose face you don't see and whose hurts you will most likely never catch a glimpse of.

It is still possible, in person, but a little more difficult.

Eye to eye, you see the passion, the gentleness, the uncertainty, the need . . . and you might tailor your responses to suit.

Because you understand they are more than just their opinions, more than just their argument.

I spent two weeks recently in the company of someone I have had the most awful online arguments with. All the subjects we fell out over never once came up.

Partly, we were keeping the peace, but mostly, I hope, being in each other's company reminded us both that we didn't actually want to hurt each other.

Frank and his mum had a series of really hurtful

iStock.

By David McLaughlan

162

▶ arguments that led to them not talking for years.

Eventually, she went into hospital for palliative care. By then, he was sure the relationship was irretrievably broken.

Days before she died, she surprised him by phoning. But she was confused, on serious medication.

She asked Frank if he knew where his mum was.

He cried as he said, "Oh, she'll be out helping someone, somewhere. Because that's what she's like. She's a lovely woman, my mum."

She believed she was right in the argument until the end, and Frank still knows he was right, but in those last hours, he moved past all that, because there were more important things!

We forget that when we are separated.

The things that separate us are usually as nothing compared to what might unite us, the common experiences that should bring us together.

Understanding that at the end, Frank had to at least try to make things better.

No-one (who mattered) did that for Andy.

We left the beach for the supermarket, where I bought him some necessities, then saw him into emergency accommodation. He died a few weeks later.

His family heard the news from strangers. Sometimes we leave it too late.

So what are we divided over? Politics? Health matters? Religion? Nationalism? Would any one of them — or all of them together — have made that sunset more or less beautiful?

Do they soothe our loneliness or make being loved more intense? Do they bring inner peace, contentment, happiness?

On some practical matters, like food and shelter, politics should make a difference. Some churches, I am sure, do make a difference.

But what is left when politics and religion fail? You and me, that's what. And the question of division.

On the one side there will be someone who was once a baby, who needed nothing more than love and shelter; someone who will win and lose, who will know joy and grief, who likes a sunset.

And on the other side is the same. In between the two, there is over-inflated trivia; things that seem so important — but won't hold your hand when you need it.

Years ago, I visited a Salvation Army hostel looking for my brother.

I had to wait a while in a day-room full of people who had been sleeping on the streets, people with addiction problems.

They swore at me, assured me I wasn't getting their biscuits, and wouldn't make space for me to sit.

But when my brother arrived, and they saw us reunited, we were embraced in the smelliest group hug ever.

What made the difference, I realised afterwards, was that every one of them was hoping, beyond their hopelessness, that someone would step over whatever their division was, and come and claim them back from the world.

I saw Andy into one hostel in mid-December and I left the other, at the same point in a different year, with my brother.

Both occurred in the run-up to Christmas, a time when we make a great deal of celebrating a baby being born.

They are blessed celebrations indeed, where someone isn't missing.

And the longer we stay apart, the less chance there is of the wound healing.

If we would have it be different, and, always, if it is safe, we might be the one who steps over the unimportant stuff and brings someone back.

Wits used to advise people going for interviews to imagine the interviewers in their underwear.

Taking away the superficial differences in clothing helped the interviewees see that they are not so different from us. After all, we all wear underwear, don't we?

If it helps, imagine the person on the other side of the divide as the baby they were and almost certainly still are at some deeper level.

Then, take the advice of the baby whose birth we celebrate each year at Christmas, perhaps the most powerful words he ever uttered when he came into his maturity.

"Love one another, as I have loved you!" ▧

Nature's Calendar For *Winter*

Early Frogspawn

In milder parts of the country, such as Cornwall, it's not uncommon for frogs to spawn earlier than spring. Over recent years there have been instances of some gambling on a mild winter and spawning in October and November. Most will wait till winter starts to wind up, with female frogs laying up to 4,000 eggs each.

In Season: Carrots

Packed with fibre, Vitamin A and beta-carotene, carrots are a hardy staple veg.

They can lead to children turning slightly orange if they eat too many, with a harmless condition called carotenemia. They're thought to originate from Afghanistan, where we began cultivating them 5,000 years ago.

Tree Life: Bare Skin

With the leaves gone, the trees no longer have to pump water to maintain them, and the tree withdraws into dormancy. New growth is almost non-existent, and it's surviving off reserves, much as animals do in hibernation. Sugars (in sap form) go down to the roots to keep the tree alive, and to protect from the weather.

Shutterstock.

In Season: Spring Onions

Ready to eat just eight weeks after sowing, spring onions are a quick, healthy choice. Milder than white onions, they're often eaten raw. If the strength disagrees with you, soak in iced or cold water for a while before using – it'll reduce their potency. You can also use the trimmed roots to grow a fresh batch by leaving them upright in water.

On The Farm: Weaning Calves

It's time for the calves to be weaned on the farm on to other feeds than mother's milk. Mothers will discourage year-old calves from coming for milk by pushing them away, letting newborns have access instead, or leaving more energy for the pregnant mums. Farmers are finding later weaning reduces stress on the calves.

Veganuary

Could you go vegan for a whole month? Veganuary encourages us to try going animal-free for the good of our health and the planet. Recipes are widely available online, but you might be surprised how easy it is to find alternatives for your regular foods. It's always good to expand your recipe repertoire.

Driving Past Memories

Barriers have been put in place,
Where the road ahead is closed,
Diverting me down country lanes,
Unwittingly imposed.

But as I take this rural route,
My mind remembers when
The two of us once walked here,
As I see it now, again.

There's the stile that led us through
The meadow to Home Wood,
Here's the pond where ducks still swim,
And where we often stood.

Ahead, beyond the hawthorn hedge,
The Penn Hills reach their peak;
We'd lie upon the stunted grass,
Feeling happy and unique.

I've not been here for many years,
Yet still I know each place,
And see, today, as I did then,
Your young and lovely face.

John Darley

Friends

A reason, a season, a lifetime,
What kind of friend are you?
The answer is not too important,
As long as your friendship is true.
For I've had my share of fair-weather friends,
They just came along for the ride,
But when things turned bad along life's way,
They disappeared like the tide.
And I've had my share of seasonal friends,
Who came along for a reason,
But faded away when the need was gone,
Just like the change in the season.
And then there are friends of a lifetime,
With me through good times and bad,
There to remind me, when life is cruel,
That things won't always be sad.
So, a reason, a season, a lifetime,
What kind of friend are you?
The answer you'll see is not important,
As long as your friendship is true.

Cherie Kemp

Road Of Life

I see the road go climbing
And winding up the hill.
I've seen it many times before,
And yet it beckons still.
I see the river flowing by,
The houses in between,
The trees and bushes beautiful,
The meadows so serene.

Is this like life? I ask myself,
Our road still winding on,
To look around and seek the sun,
When darker days have gone.
Sometimes the way is rough and steep,
We have a heavy load,
But make the most of every day
On life's great winding road!

Iris Hesselden

"Love is a fruit in season at all times, and within reach of every hand."
— Mother Teresa